THE SUPER SITE PROCESS

HOW TO CREATE A HIGHLY PROFITABLE WEBSITE FOR YOUR SMALL BUSINESS

MICHAEL H PURVIS

CONTENTS

"Paying attention to simple little things that most men neglect makes a few men rich."

– HENRY FORD

INTRODUCTION

Hello. My name is Mike Purvis. I'm one of the founding partners of NH Strategic Marketing. My business partner, Kyle Battis, and I launched the business way back in 2012. We started this business to have a more direct impact in our local community.

We had both been independently contracting for online companies whose entire income was generated through the internet - businesses making $5M - $10M a year. These were *real* businesses that employed real people - and whose livelihood depended on results. And this meant staying ahead of the curve and on top of what worked online. Because way back then, the 'rules' for internet marketing changed on a week to week basis.

Interestingly, we had an opportunity to apply some of what we had learned in scaling these internet based businesses to a few local 'brick and mortar' businesses (requests from family and friends), and we were shocked at how much *better* these strategies worked with offline businesses! Time and time again, when we applied what was working for fully online companies, to offline companies, the results were nothing short of amazing.

After seeing the impact we were having on these small businesses and the livelihoods of the owners and their people, we decided to go all in with helping small businesses grow through smart online marketing.

I won't bore you tooting our own horn; after all, this book is about YOUR business , not ours. But I also understand, trust must be earned. If this is your first run-in with us, I'll encourage you to take a couple of minutes to check out our reputation online. We have 5 Star ratings on Google and Facebook and an A+ rating with the Better Business Bureau. You'll see we've been at this a long time; we're passionate about what we do; and we care about our clients and their businesses. We have a ton of client testimonials on our website (NHStrategicMarketing.com), and if you're local to our office in Concord, NH then you can probably just ask around to see what the other local businesses think of us. Our company motto is "Do the right thing." And it's what guides us in every decision we make, and through all work we do for, and with our clients.

Our clients are rock stars, and we love seeing their eyes light up when they really start to 'get it'. We work with them to turn their websites into real, profit-producing assets for the company – a 24x7 salesperson who is always on, representing the business in a positive light, and driving revenue - that's the key. Because your website (and related assets), can (and should), be your single biggest source of new business – period.

If it's not, then read on to discover how to fix it!

1

WHY INVESTING IN A TYPICAL
WEBSITE IS A BAD IDEA

Let's face it, the old ways of building websites just aren't cutting it anymore.

We talk with a LOT of business owners each month, and I'm always shocked at how many of them look at their website as a pain in the butt, or something they only deal with because they feel they have to. If you've ever caught yourself thinking something like this, then the time we spend together here, will definitely change the course of your business in a massively positive way.

There's one thing that many (if not all), of the most successful businesses today realize. It's why they're as busy as they want to be. And why they never lay awake at night worrying about the future of their business.

They understand that a business website can (and should), become your single largest, most predictable, most scalable, and most affordable source of new customers – period. Bigger than any offline source, and more effective than even word of mouth referrals. But there's a caveat. And it's that this is only true if your website is designed from the ground up to be a high converting sales machine.

Most are not.

Pretty websites make people feel good – but they won't grow your business. Most website design companies are only focused on appearances – not on the more important elements that will actually drive new business. And this trend has left many business owners with a sour taste in their mouths.

If you want a website designed to grow your business, then I'm going to share with you how we approach website design. Although our model is completely 'against the grain' from traditional web design companies, our clients love us for it. Because when you design your site around the five core concepts I'm going to share with you here, your website will not only look nice, it will quickly become your most prized sales machine. It will do the job it was meant to do.

If you're still thinking your website isn't really that important, I'd encourage you to pause and consider these sobering facts:

1. "97% of consumers go online to find a local business or local services." So in other words – *everyone* uses the internet to find a local company to do business with. That's huge!

2. "Up to 80% of people RESEARCH a company online before visiting or making a purchase with them." So that means that the majority of those people searching you out online are digging deeper to find out more about you *before* giving you their business.

So that means that the majority of your would-be, future customers are going *online* looking for someone to help them before picking up the phone or heading to a store. And I can tell you (and you probably know from your own search behaviors) – nobody searches beyond page one of Google. So you need a website strategy designed to keep your site showing up on page one for searches related to the products and services you offer.

Because no matter how pretty your website is – if it doesn't show up on page one when people are looking – nobody is going to see it.

So what does this mean?

Well, basically it means that when it comes to building out an EFFECTIVE website, you need to put the majority of your effort into preliminary research, marketing and strategy – not design. Don't get me wrong, appearance is important (it's really important). But it still pales in comparison to the other elements involved in building out a web presence that will grow your business.

I'm going to share with you the five key areas we walk our clients through when planning and launching their web presence. Notice I didn't say 'building a website' – because a website, although an integral part of the plan, is not the ENTIRE plan. It's a core component, but it's *not* the whole.

Think of your website exactly as you would a physical store or shop. It's just like real estate in the 'real world'; only this real estate is on the internet. So, you know you need to have an attractive storefront. Well, this would be the same as your website's homepage.

The inside of your store needs to be organized and easy to browse as well. This would correlate to the additional pages of your website.

And with your offline business, when people need help or want to do business with you, someone needs to be available to help them. And you need to make it easy to do business with you. It's the same with your website. How easy is it for people to contact you through your website, or to purchase from you online, etc.

Most everyone can understand the importance of having an attractive, easy to use website. Just like you know your physical location needs to be inviting. And this is where most web design companies focus - building attractive websites.

So, remembering that your online presence (your website), is essentially the same thing as a physical business, let me ask you:

How successful would your business be if nobody could find you? If all you did was set up shop (albeit a beautiful shop), and wait for the phone to ring. What if you set up shop on a new road that wasn't even on GPS? What if you didn't promote and market your business offline? And what if - even for the people that did stumble across your business – you made it difficult for them to contact you, or the person answering your phones couldn't give them clear information about what you do and why you're better than the countless other options out there? How long would you be in business?

Not very long.

The problem is that most small businesses treat their websites exactly like this. They know they have to *have* a website, so they invest in getting one. But the site is most often built by designers, without input or direction from anyone with online sales and marketing expertise. Without someone who knows about conversion elements. Without anyone doing the hard (but critically important), work of flushing out the competition, and establishing a unique position for the business online. Because the fact is, there's a lot of competition online in almost all markets. But the *online* competition is quite possibly different than your *offline* competition. So you need someone who knows how to dig into this stuff if you want to get results.

You need to make sure your website can get found. You need someone to make sure visitors who are looking for the products and services you offer, see YOUR website when they search online.

None of this happens magically. It all has to be thought out, and built into your online strategy. And much of it has to do with how your website is built, structured and promoted.

That's exactly why we don't just build websites.

We create highly visible, conversion focused web properties designed to grow your small business.

We lovingly call these properties Super Sites, and they will dramatically change the course of your business for the better.

We go through a five stage process with all of our Super Site clients, and in the following pages, I'm going to walk you step-by-step through the key elements of our process. You'll quickly realize why most small business websites aren't doing the work they should be, and why deploying a Super Site for your business will quickly turn the Internet into your favorite new customer acquisition channel.

So... let's get started.

HOW TO GUARANTEE EXPLOSIVE GROWTH FOR YOUR BUSINESS BY USING THE INTERNET THE RIGHT WAY

Is a Super Site really just a super-charged website?

No. It's an online SYSTEM with a website at its core. The website is built in a very different way (intentionally so), and is designed to convert many more visitors into customers, sure. But what's exponentially more important is the 'front end' of the system - the work that goes into making sure your site actually gets found. The work that goes into making sure your business is positioned above your competition (both physically in search results *and* from a marketing perspective). And all of the other things that happen BEFORE someone ever reaches your website. This is where a huge part of the Super Site magic happens.

You need to stop thinking about your website as a stand alone thing. It's actually just a *part* of your online business. A very integral part. It's where people go to learn more about you; to contact you; to compare you to the competition etc. - but some of the most important elements of an effective online strategy happen long before a visitor lands on your website.

And not to get too far ahead of myself here, but there's also the 'back end' of your website strategy; which is what happens when people visit, but then leave your site. Believe it or not, these are some of your best opportunities (if you're using a Super Site, and remarketing properly to these potential new customers). Your website does the work of 'tagging' these people, but you also have to 'connect' some other systems to make sure these people keep seeing you everywhere (even when they visit your competitors). You've experienced the power of remarketing yourself hundreds of times no doubt. Ever go to someone's website and look at their products, only to realize you start seeing ads for them everywhere else you go online? That's the power of effective remarketing, and it can change your business (if you do it properly and have a high converting website as part of your online strategy).

Here's another massive problem facing small businesses today: when it comes to their internet presence, most small businesses build their websites and promote themselves online *without* considering the competitive landscape, or taking into account what their ideal prospects are already seeing, and what data they're using to make a buying decision. They have no idea how they're being 'compared' to all of the other options their ideal prospects have to choose from.

And this is a real problem!

Let me explain.

If you get one thing from this chapter, let it be this:

The internet is NOT an unlimited source of new business. Sure, it's much more scalable than a local geography, and you can reach ten times as many people for a fraction of the marketing investment compared to offline, but you have to realize:

There are only so many people searching online each
month for the products and/or services you offer.

It is a LIMITED inventory, and the businesses who
capture the greatest market share, for the smallest investment,
will win - plain and simple

So when it comes to being found, your goal should always
be two-fold.

First, you have to get in front of as many people as possible
who are looking for the products and/or services you offer each
and every month. This is called 'impression share'. Every time
you show up when someone searches a keyword related to your
business, you get a chance to compete. And remember, there
are only so many chances available each month. And there are
only so many 'spaces' available in the placements that matter
(like page one of Google). Typically only 3-4 businesses get to
compete on front page placements. You want to be one of them.
Otherwise your website might as well not even exist. This is the
all-important 'front end' work I was talking about earlier. You
have to be *seen* before you can win.

And second, you want to work toward paying less than
your competition for higher (more valuable), placements.
When it comes to Google - the higher placements always
generate more traffic (visitors), to your website. A lot of people
think that you have to pay more to place higher - but that's
simply not true. Google's most important goal is to provide their
users (the searchers), with the best experience possible. They
know that if they provide an amazing search experience, the
users will keep coming back to Google. Pretty simple right?
The good news for you is that a Super Site is designed to
provide an *amazing* user experience.

Google watches for 'signals' from users who visit a website - and they use these signals to tell if your website provides a good experience or not. Some signals include: was the website secure, was it fast loading, and mobile friendly etc., but more importantly, did the visitor find what they were looking for (meaning they didn't 'bounce' or return back to the search results); did they 'convert' on your site etc. When Google sees that your site gives visitors exactly what they were looking for, they reward you (handsomely), with higher placements.

And when it comes to pay-per-click services (like Google Ads), you'll often pay much less per visitor than your competition. All because your site provides the best user experience.

User experience is that important to Google, and so it should be for you too.

Ok, so we've just roughly touched on the importance of front-end strategy and back-end strategy; and of course, right there in the middle, is your website.

So many businesses try jumping right to the middle; "let's build a website!", and they completely miss the boat. You can't build an *effective* website without dialing in your entire strategy *first*. Splintered marketing rarely works. And when it works at all, it's extremely ineffective, and unnecessarily expensive.

Remember, the goal should never be to 'get a website built' - it should be: "How can we create a consistent, reliable, and cost effective 24x7 sales machine for our business. And the good news - it's not as hard (or expensive), as you might think.

Let's start with a 30k foot view of the stages we go through in the Super Site process.

We'll go into greater detail in the following chapters of course, but here's a brief overview of key stages (and don't worry, we'll walk you through how to assess and perform each of the items at each stage, step-by-step, in future chapters):

1. Technical Planning and Strategic Research: I'll show you how to uncover your competitor's most effective marketing strategies so you can beat them at their own game.
2. Clarifying Your Messaging and Call To Action: Together we'll uncover the 'magical words' that will ensure prospects choose you every time, and we'll make sure they take the *exact* action you want them to when visiting your site.
3. Designing, Deploying and Optimizing Your New Website: Building your 'Super Site' - all of the things you didn't even know you don't know :) We'll walk you through all of the steps we use ourselves when building out our client's sites.
4. Launching Critical Visibility Campaigns: How to make sure your ideal customers see your site everywhere it matters - every time. This is the start of leveraging your new site into business growth!
5. Reviewing Results And Scaling: Moving toward market domination (or just making a bunch more money - your choice).

We see a lot of business owners get 'stuck' when making decisions on the above items. Or worse, skipping the most important ones entirely! Don't worry, I won't let that happen to you.

My only word of caution would be to watch for yourself saying something like: "Oh, I already know about that." Because in many cases, we don't know what we don't know. Take the time to follow our process to the letter and you'll be amazed at how much clarity you'll have in knowing that you're moving forward in a direction of greater results and profit for your business.

Ok, so that's the 30k foot view of the process. Let's jump right in to Stage 1 and see how to launch your business toward exponential growth - brought to you by... proper research!

"Building a business website without first looking at the competitive landscape, is like building your dream house in a neighborhood you know nothing about. It's just a bad idea."

- MIKE PURVIS

3

HOW TO REVEAL YOUR COMPETITORS MOST EFFECTIVE MARKETING STRATEGIES AND BEAT THEM AT THEIR OWN GAME

The first and most important thing you can do when planning your website - is a complete and thorough competitor analysis.

If we compare building your business website to building your dream-house - think of this part of the process as the 'Where and Why' of house planning. When building your dream house, you don't just start nailing boards together - right?

Of course not.

The first thing you do is decide (very strategically), *where* you want to live - and *why* you want to live there. You research the weather, the neighbors, the school systems, the tax rates and a hundred other data points before deciding on *where* to build. The where always comes before the what (or at least it should :)

Can you imagine investing a million dollars or more into building a dream-house for your family, only to later realize that you built it on a fault line; in a town whose school system was one of the lowest rated schools in the country; and in a region subject to dangerous tornadoes, and with a high crime rate? Would that be a problem for you? Of course it would!

Your amazing new home just became a massive liability - not the life changing improvement you were hoping for.

Your website is exactly the same. Build your website without doing a proper competitive analysis - or without doing a handful of other key things first - and all of that investment of time, energy and money you put into your site will lead to massive disappointment - and zero growth for your business.

Do this research and setup properly however, and you'll be poised to immediately capture more market share for your business - leaving your competition wondering: "What just happened - where have all our new customers gone?"

You do remember our earlier point about there being a limited number of potential new customers online each month right? Well it's time for you to get more of them for yourself!

In the 'Technical Planning and Strategic Research' phase of our Super Site build out, we're going to go through the following exercises that will set you up for immediate and long term success - eventually making your business untouchable online:

1. First, we're going to figure out *exactly* what you want to be found for online. You can't be number one for everything (at least not right away), so in this exercise we're going to figure out which battles you want to win right out of the gate, and which search queries are likely to mean the most to your business's bottom line *today*.

2. Next, we're going to do a full analysis of your competition's current marketing strategies. We'll not only see what they're doing - but much more importantly, we'll be able to uncover what's working to drive new business for them. We'll figure out where they're showing up, and how

they're positioning themselves in your market. This data will be critical to the future success of YOUR website and overall online presence.

3. We'll then take some time to do a reputation assessment of your business *and* your competition's. Your online reputation is a huge factor in your ability to compete online. And don't worry - if you do have some issues (like less than stellar reviews or star ratings), we have strategies to help.

This will also be the time to think about any third party tools your business relies on - such as your Customer Relationship Management tools, and other add-ons you may want to incorporate into your website to make driving engagement, lead flow and sales easier, and more effective. I'll cover that in a bit more detail at the end of this section, but let's get into the fun stuff first :)

Real quickly - before we get into the core of this, I want to talk about your domain name.

If you already have a website and are just revamping - this won't come into play. But if you're launching your site, or you're a brand new business, you may be struggling with picking a domain name. Here's my best advice: keep it simple, and don't over think it.

Here are the simple rules our team follows when choosing domain names for our clients. These rules are based on seeing results across thousands of domain names and in hundreds of different business markets:

1. If you can get yourbusinessname.com - that's what you want to use. Don't use an abbreviation, unless

it's very memorable or your business name is crazy long. Your domain name will act as a branding mechanism, and you want people to remember your business name - not an abbreviation.

2. If you can't get yourbusinessname.com - I would still stick with a .com for 99% of businesses. I won't get into the exceptions here, but if your a typical B2B or B2C business, then you should stick with a dot com. So in this case, figure out how to easily 'add on' to your business name in a memorable way. As an example: if you're a NH based business, you could get yourbusinessnamenh.com. Easy enough. State initials are a great way to secure a business name domain when the regular businessname.com is already taken - and it's easy for your customers to remember.

3. Just make sure you can say your domain out loud without having to explain it to someone - and if you do *have* to get one that requires some clarification, you're better off buying any potentially confusing domain variations and redirecting them all to your main domain. Here's an example: Let's say your business name is '4 Seasons Landscaping LLC'. If you registered 4seasonslandscaping.com you might also want to register fourseasonslandscaping.com so you don't have to tell people "It's the number 4, and then seasonslandscaping.com".

And that's about all you need to know about choosing a domain name. There are hundreds of domain suppliers out there, but I'd recommend just going to GoDaddy.com and register there. It's a very simple process.

Ok, now that we have that out of the way - let's jump in to the fun stuff.

We'll start with determining what you want to be found for.

You need to begin your website build out by asking yourself one very important question:

"What are the most important search terms I want my website to be found for?"

In other words – what is your primary product and/or service?

What terms would you absolutely want to be certain you show up on page one for when someone searches for them?

As an example, a roofing company in Concord, NH would most likely want to make sure they rank for 'roofing company concord nh' and similar search terms. This is so important, and most small businesses never start with getting clear on this. There are a lot of factors that go into getting found for a specific search query, and your website framework is a huge factor.

So backing up for a moment - in case you're asking: "What is a search query?"

Anytime you go to Google - or more specifically, anytime you open a web browser (Chrome, Firefox, Safari etc.), and you perform a search - the words you type in represent a 'search query'.

Nowadays, over 60% of searches are done on smartphones, and our browsers (even on desktop and laptop devices), take our location and search history into account when delivering results. So in the above example (roofing company concord nh), we wouldn't even need to add 'concord nh' to the search query - we could just search for 'roofer near me' (which is a more typical search), and Google will only show results local to us. Search engines are smart - really smart :)

But when we're planning out what we want to show up for, we need to plan on the full search queries, because we're going to need to 'feed' Google the info it needs to determine our service areas etc.

When designing the initial plan for the site it's important to *really* focus in on the search terms that are most likely to lead to new customers and revenue for your business. It takes a lot of effort (and sometimes a financial investment), to set yourself up to show for each search term, so you don't want to tackle too much right out of the gate. You also don't want to 'confuse' the search engines by trying to position yourself as the expert for 10 different services. Over time you can start to rank and show up for many more keyword categories; but initially, we encourage our clients to decide on the top 1-3 products or services that mean the most to their business. What are you the absolute best at. What are the 2-3 cornerstone products/services for your business? Take the time to answer these questions specifically.

Let's stick with the roofer example above. In this case, their core service keywords might revolve around 'metal roofing', 'roof repair', 'residential roofing'. Now they might also do gutters, ventilation, storm damage, and even siding; but you have to pick your core services FIRST. So, feed the search engines everything they need to know you're the go-to company in your area for the core services you offer, and later you can build out rankings for your other services. It's worth repeating:

You need to build out credibility and clarity for your core business services first.

Businesses that try to show up for every service they offer (or for every product they sell), right out of the gate never win. We've seen this time and time again. Businesses launch a new site and haven't FOCUSED their initial efforts on a single category or topic. Everything they do is watered down, and results are mediocre at best.

You'll see the importance of picking your battles, and why it becomes exponentially more important as we go into future stages of the Super Site Process. As an example, we're going to move into doing a competitor analysis next. Knowing that, let me ask you: for our example company... do you think the competitors for their roofing services (metal roofing, roof repair, residential roofing), are the same as their competitors for 'gutters'?

Most likely not.

When they want to start 'owning' the gutter market, they'll need to jump back in and do another round of competitor analysis for this category. That will involve some additional keyword research; reputation assessments for their competitors; offer analysis for the new competitors; and all of the other steps we'll discuss here. They'd likely need some additional dedicated pages for the 'gutter' services and would need to create competitive offers and points of differentiation etc.

This is an entirely separate battle.

Trying to win in every area of your business all at once is a recipe for disappointment. We've launched a LOT of websites and businesses, and I can tell you; I've seen very few companies that have the mental bandwidth or capacity to build out an effective online marketing presence for more than 1-2 key areas of their business at once.

Ok, so choosing your target and related keywords is fairly simple - just put yourself in your prospective customer's shoes and think about the terms people will type in to find you (for the core products/services you've decided on). Make a list of the top 5-10 keywords. That's all you'll need for the moment.

Now, when we do this for clients, we have a few different tools we use that give us insights about actual search volumes for the keywords we're planning on targeting. Ideally, you only want to target the highest volume keywords for your market and geography. Building a business around keywords that have little (or no), search volume is a terrible strategy. One tool you can use to get some useful keyword data as part of this process is ahrefs.com. It's not inexpensive, but you don't want to launch your online business without getting this part right!

We can also help you with this research and making sure you're moving in the right direction. Just reach out to us on our website at NHStrategicMarketing.com

Ok, so once you have this, it's time to figure out who and/or what you're up against.

Let's do some competitor analysis!

So... how exactly *do* you see what your competitors are currently doing to drive results and stay in front of your best prospects and customers? And more importantly, how do you reverse engineer it and do it better?

Well, it's not as difficult as you might think.

As an agency, we have a number of tools that we use to get highly accurate reports on a competitor's organic traffic and their paid ad campaigns. We can even get detailed reports to see what they're doing on social channels, and how all of their listings across the web (on things like directory sites), are set up etc.

For those that are interested, a few tools that are available publicly are WhatRunsWhere, SpyFu and Ahrefs. These are just a few examples, and honestly, I wouldn't recommend the average business owner investing in such services. Not because of the monetary cost, but more importantly because of the time that you'll lose learning how to properly use them. And unless you're an online advertising pro, there are many ways you can also easily misinterpret the information - and as you can imagine, that could have seriously negative effects when launching your site.

I only share them here, because I'm always asked for suggestions on research tools, and I don't want to hold anything back.

But the good news is, you can do a pretty decent job of getting a good chunk of competitor insights *without* the expensive tools and insider access.

Here's how to do a simple analysis following the 80/20 rule.

First, grab your keyword list. Go to Google and start searching - just like your ideal prospect would. Simply type in your keywords one at a time and see what results come up.

A very important note here: Make sure Google isn't using your search or account history in any way to tailor search results. Keeping in mind that Google tries to provide the absolute best user experience possible, they're going to show you search results as they pertain specifically to you. And for this case we don't want that.

We want to know what results get returned for a typical user - not for us specifically.

You can do that by searching in an 'incognito' window. The easiest way to learn how to do this (if you don't already know), is to do a Google search for 'how to search incognito in chrome' and follow the instructions. It only takes two seconds, but this will ensure we get *real* results.

Okay, so you've typed in your first search query and have the page one results.

There are typically a few separate sections on page one. They'll vary by industry - but for the majority of businesses we work with the areas of focus are:

1. The top of page Google Ads listings. These are paid ads - otherwise known as PPC or Pay Per Click ads. Not all search queries will have these ads, but most keywords that will lead to new business do. The types and number of ads vary, and Google is always experimenting with new ad types etc., but look for the little 'Ad' label next to the listings and you'll know they're paid ads. Google also runs ads at the bottom of the page too.

2. Below the top Google Ads listings are normally the Maps or Business listings (for those industries that support Maps listings - not all do, but most local businesses do). You'll recognize these placements are currently separated out in their own area, and there are usually only three or so businesses listed on page one, and a link to 'view more', that leads to a page to see the other local businesses.

3. Below the Maps listings are the Organic Placements. These are businesses or content pieces Google feels are most relevant to your search query. Not all of them will be direct competition for you (unlike the Ads and Maps listings), but there's no doubt you'll find some competition in here as well.

4. Now, if you are selling e-commerce or physical products, there will also be Google Shopping ads at the top of the page, and potentially in other areas of the page as well. For the purpose of this book, we're going to be focusing primarily on local and service based businesses and their websites, so we won't go too deep on e-commerce strategy, but many of the principles we discuss here certainly apply. We do a lot of work with e-commerce brands, so feel free to

reach out to us directly with any questions that come up as you read through the book.

Ok, so you have your search results pulled up in an incognito window for your first search query - great!

Take note (literally), of the companies that are running paid ads. Check out the copy (text), for their ads. What special offers, incentives, or points of differentiation are they highlighting? Visit the url from the ad.

Note: the advertisers have to pay for clicks on their ads, so you want to do everything you can to get to their destination pages without clicking their ads. Open a new tab and visit each of the display urls to see what their landing pages look like and what user experience they provide. See what offers they make, and take note of how they position themselves.

Are they providing a good offer that is directly related to the search query and related ad? Do they have good social proof (testimonials, ratings etc.), on their page? Do they make it easy to contact them? Is the site secure, modern and mobile focused, etc.?

All of this matters - a lot.

We're basically trying to get a view of the competitive landscape here. You want to see exactly what your prospective customers are going to see - and you want to make sure that you position yourself above the crowd. It's not easy - but it's necessary if you want to win. And you're reading this book, so I'm fairly certain you want to win :)

Take notes about each experience for each advertiser in the Google Ads listings at the top of the page, and then at the bottom. Make sure to list them in order (1,2,3 etc.), as the advertisers closer to the top of the page are the ones that matter most.

When it comes to page one search results, the farther down the page your business is, the less traffic you receive.

As an example - when it comes to these paid listings, the top placement (position one), will typically receive more clicks (visits to your website from these ads), than positions two and three *combined*! So as you can see - position matters. Especially since we now know that there are only so many searches each month for our products and/or services. We want (need), to capture as many of these clicks (visits), as possible.

Now do the same type of research for the Maps listings. Just note the companies that are on page one. We won't worry too much about those that are on the page after you click the 'More Businesses' link. Not at the moment anyway - we'll investigate these businesses more when we look at scaling in the future. For those on page one, take note of the business name, how many reviews they have, their websites, hours, etc. This is your competition in the Maps section.

And finally do the same bit of research for the Organic listings (all listings between the maps listings, and the lower Ads).

Now you should have a detailed list of all your page one competition for this first keyword.

In many cases, you'll find the same competitor will have placements in multiple places (Google Ads, Maps *and* Organic listings - or any combination of these). These are the businesses who are most likely to be crushing it with their internet presence and who are driving *real* business from their site.

This should be *your* goal as well!

Our goal for every client we represent is to own the highest position in all three placements. In this way, you'll be capturing the maximum number of new customers month after month.

A couple of points:

1. Always open links in a new tab (right click the link

with your mouse and select 'open link in new tab'). Otherwise your core search results will update each time you go 'back', and your results will be skewed.

2. Only do one keyword search at a time in a single incognito window. Then close the browser (Chrome), and reopen it. Then open another incognito window before doing the next keyword search. You want to make sure Google isn't using your search behavior during the research for one keyword, and skewing results for the next one.

Follow the process above for each of your core keywords and document everything in a simple spreadsheet - each keyword results in its own sheet.

Now, in a new sheet, list who you see as your top 3-5 online competitors.

Who showed up the most, and the best? Who had a 'made me want to call them over us' website / online presence? Who had the best offer etc.?

This is who/what you're up against. Now you know what your ideal prospects are currently seeing, you'll be in a perfect position to make sure *your* website stands out above the crowd.

I see way too many businesses stick their heads in the sand and actually avoid doing this type of research - probably because they know they won't like what they see.

But here's the reality:

This is the absolute best thing you can do for your business if you want a website and online presence that will drive new business. If you want things to stay exactly as they are - then ignore this. You'll be ok for a little while. Maybe a year or two more. But by then it will be too late for you to catch up, and you'll have lost.

I don't want this happening to your business. Get out in front of this today.

You'll thank me later - I'm sure of it.

And if you ever get overwhelmed with any of this - remember: this is what we do , day in and day out. Visit our website or give us a call - we can help.

Oh, and there's one more area of competitive research I just want to touch on real quick, and that's reputation.

Now's the time to do an honest assessment of your online reputation - meaning: do people get an immediate sense of trust when they see you online - and does it look like more people do business with *you* over anyone else.

There are two important factors to consider when looking at a business online. It's the same as looking at product reviews on Amazon. When your prospects are trying to decide who to call or visit (and eventually do business with), they're going to look at your star ratings on Google and Facebook, and they're going to check out any other relevant reviews they see online that are from third parties. Testimonials and reviews on your own site are ok - but we generally don't trust it when a yet unknown source tells us they're great. We want to see it from an unbiased, well known and trusted third-party - like Google.

So ultimately, you want to make sure you have the highest star rating of any of your competition on the main platforms for your business. The Google Business Listings in the center of page one are one of the most important places reviews show for many of the businesses we work with. You need to encourage reviews from your happy customers here as it will make a *huge* difference for the future of your business.

The recency of reviews is important, but most important of all (besides the actual rating itself - for example, 4.5 or 5 stars), is the number of reviews. You want to have many more positive reviews than your competition. And in most businesses we work with - this is an easy thing to do. Your prospects will compare the number of reviews for your business against your competition and assume that whoever has the most reviews is trusted by the most people - so they must be the best choice.

In many cases having a higher volume of positive reviews is even more important than a higher position on the page. As we view the page one results, our eyes are immediately drawn to the yellow star ratings - and we start drawing conclusions and making decisions about who to pick before we ever read another word, or click a link.

Your online reputation is a huge part of the Super Site process for a few reasons, but the biggest is this: when people search you out online, and they see you have the greatest quality and number of reviews - before they even land on your site - they're coming in with a much greater level of trust and confidence in your business. Because of this, they're exponentially closer to being ready to give you their business than a visitor who hasn't seen that social proof - or who saw social proof that was less than the best.

So, look at the ratings for your own business, as well as the ratings of the competitors we outlined earlier, and make a game plan for working toward having the most (and best), ratings in your competitive landscape. You can do this by asking your best customers to leave a review about their experience with your business, and you should make this 'ask for a review' step part of your core experience.

Sometimes it can be difficult to remember to ask for an online review from your customers. And it can be even more difficult, walking them through how to leave that review on Google, and other platforms. But it's worth it, I assure you.

As you might imagine, there are tools that we can set up to

help automate this process for your business. This makes the process a little easier for small business owners that may not have staff dedicated to making sure this important work is being done.

And with automation, you also have a chance to get in front of any 'less-than-perfect' reviews; to have the opportunity to correct an issue before a poor review is left. Negative reviews can be very damaging to a business, and as you probably know, it can take many 5 star reviews to offset a single poor review.

Whether you choose to invest in a review management system, or you do it manually, doesn't matter. What matters, is that you put a focus on your online reputation and leverage it as a part of your Super Site system.

Ok, so you've done the competitive research; and you have a handle on what needs to be done as far as your online reputation.

There are just a couple of other decisions to make at this stage. Let's get into those now.

There are a lot of 'tools' you may want to consider using on your website. We've dealt with integrating hundreds of different features into our client's sites to make them more effective at driving revenue for the business.

You'll need to consider your customer relationship management system (CRM), for capturing and nurturing leads - of course. But you may also have a few other tools you want to integrate. Maybe you want to be able to offer gift cards on your site. There's a system for that.

Or maybe you want to allow people to make a reservation, or to book online. There are tools for that as well.

Or maybe you want to offer live chat for visitors on specific pages of your site. There are a dozen different options for that as well.

For just about anything you can think of - there are tools already built to get set up quickly and easily.

The sheer volume of softwares designed to help small business websites convert more visitors into customers is staggering. It's a multi-*billion* dollar industry.

But I always advise our clients to be very thoughtful and careful when considering what add-ons to integrate with their site. With each system you integrate, you are adding additional cost, complexity and possible confusion for your users - so you want to be very intentional with your choices.

As we dive in here, it's important to keep in mind that what makes a website a conversion-machine is rarely the 'bells and whistles', or some cutting edge software - it's more often the positioning; the work on the front-end systems (like your online reputation); and your back-end systems (like your traffic campaigns, follow up processes etc.). These are the things that *really* move the needle.

Website plugins and add-ons can definitely be helpful and add a bump to conversion rates, but it's these other core areas that will be responsible for the real growth in your business.

That being said, I think it might be helpful to discuss how we advise clients when looking at added features for their site.

Here are the things you need to think about and consider when choosing any third-party integration with your site:

1. Is the tool going to help you capture more leads from the site?
2. Is it going to make it easier for your prospective customers to contact you in a method that *they* prefer (by email, messenger, live chat etc.)?

3. Is it going to increase a visitor's trust in your business?
4. Is it going to make it easier for a prospect to do business with you (or give you money)?

These are the biggest questions to start with. If you have a tool that fulfills one (or more), of the goals above, these are the next set of questions to ask - to weigh out if it really makes sense to invest in the integration:

1. How much does it cost (up front, and ongoing)?
2. How difficult is it to install or set up?
3. How much ongoing maintenance might it require?
4. How steep is the learning curve?
5. How much is it really going to help grow the business - and can it be tracked?
6. How difficult will it be to *stop* using it in the future if you determine it isn't adding to your bottom line?

Asking these questions up front is a great way to save serious headaches down the line.

Weigh it all out, and once you've decided which additions you definitely want to deploy with the site build out, you can take the action of signing up for the new services and preparing things to add to the site once we get to building it out.

The point here, is that it's much more efficient to set up any new software and to familiarize yourself with how it works *before* you get too deep in the actual site build. So use this time effectively!

And that just leaves one other topic for discussion...
Email.

. . .

A lot of newer small businesses don't realize the credibility they lose when a potential customer sees their email is not domain specific - meaning an email like yourname@yourdomain.com. They try to get away with using an email from a free email provider (like Gmail), or worse, from their Internet Service Provider - like Comcast. These services are great for personal email accounts, but you shouldn't be using them for business.

Your business email needs to be attached to your domain, and it needs to be hosted through a reputable provider. We recommend and use Google's G-Suite for the majority of our clients. It's a professional level account that ensures (when set up properly), high deliverability (meaning when you send someone an email, they're likely to actually receive it), great spam protection and great flexibility with accounts.

So, very simply, when it comes to setting up your email - use G-Suite set up for your business domain.

Ok, that's everything for the first stage.

You should now have a solid grasp on the keywords you want to be found for - and who your competition is for each of them.

You should have a clear picture of everyone's online reputation (including your own), and again - you know what you need to do here.

You know what third party apps you'll want to integrate into your site, and have started getting those ready.

And you have a plan for your domain specific email.

At this point, you should have a very solid view of the competitive landscape - and I hope it's looking favorable for you as we move toward planning your website.

If it *doesn't* look great, don't worry! That's why we do this research ahead of time; so you can start the work that will move you toward becoming the market leader.

So, even if things don't look great at the moment, you now know exactly where you stand - and you're starting to learn what you need to do to win!

You know what they say: "Knowing is half the battle."

And that's the truth.

Knowing how our competition is showing up online is a great start; and you've already done more than 80% of the businesses online. The next stage is all about how to make sure your messaging is clear, and designed in a way to provide *immediate* certainty for your visitors. We want to make sure nobody that visits your site has to 'figure out what you're all about - and what you do' - because a confused mind, never buys.

So let's get to it.

4

UNCOVERING THE 'MAGICAL WORDS' THAT WILL ENSURE YOUR BEST PROSPECTS CHOOSE YOU EVERY TIME

One of the biggest issues we see time and time again with small business websites is *clarity*.

You need to make one hundred percent sure that a new visitor to your site can tell who you are, and what you do within three seconds. And that's no exaggeration.

You have to remember - a lot of work goes into making sure your website is attracting the right type of visitors. You took the time to do the research, and you know exactly *where* you need to show up and *how* you need to show up, and you know all of the other messages these visitors have seen (or will see).

So now you need to make sure that you have a more compelling reason for this visitor to choose *you*. And I can tell you without a shadow of a doubt - *clarity* trumps almost anything. Letting them know that they're in the right place, and that you not only offer the products and/or services they're in search of - but also that you're different and better. This will cause visitors to go deeper into your site. This isn't an easy task, but it's an important one.

When you visited your competitor's sites, you probably had

to dig a bit, and think a bit, to figure out exactly what they do and who they serve.

You want to make sure that a visitor to *your* site doesn't have to think. And you want to make sure they know exactly what you do, and that you can help them, by crafting a simple one-liner to go at the top of your site.

In our case, NH Strategic Marketing's one-liner is "We help small businesses grow through smart online marketing." That's it.

We know that our ideal prospect is a small business owner; we know they're looking to grow their business; we know they're interested in doing it through online marketing and increased visibility; and we know that that's *exactly* what we do and who we serve.

And because the prospect was able to immediately verify that they're in the right place, they'll stick around a little longer to see what we have to say.

A good book keeps readers attention one sentence at a time. Then one paragraph at a time - and one chapter at a time. The author knows they have to keep the reader engaged every step of the way, or they'll put the book down and never return to it.

The same is true of your website. You need to move the visitor through your story one scroll and one click at a time. Keep them engaged.

The one-liner is what allows you to grab the visitor's attention. It's like the tagline or inside cover for a book. It gives you a chance to draw your visitors in deeper.

A lot of businesses will offer many products and/or services - and it can be difficult to boil your business down to a single sentence.

Believe me, I understand. But taking the time to figure out how to say it in a sentence will be important.

NH Strategic Marketing offers a lot of services. We're a full service digital marketing agency, so we offer website design and build out, we offer marketing strategy and planning, we do search engine optimization, pay-per-click marketing like Google Ads and Microsoft Ads, we run Facebook campaigns, and a lot more. So it was difficult to figure out how to simplify that to one sentence.

Your original thought may be that you're not telling enough - and that you'll miss out on giving some of your prospects a clear picture. But don't worry - that's not the case. If you get it right, you'll hook them enough so that they know you're a good choice for what they're looking for.

Let's move back to our Four Seasons Landscaping LLC example. Let's say they do lawn maintenance, retaining walls, patios, outside fireplaces and a bunch of other amazing services. Trying to speak to all of those services in their one-liner would be overwhelming to most prospects. It certainly would not offer clarity, and it wouldn't set them apart from their competition. Because you can bet their competition is trying to tell everyone, everything.

The reality is, if someone is looking for a patio, and the first thing they see is 'lawn maintenance', they may discredit this company as a hardscaping professional. I could give a bunch of other examples, but I think you get the point.

For our example, a good one-liner might be "Landscapes So Beautiful, You'll Want To Skip The Resort Vacation And Stay Home" or "We Build Dream Yards" or "We Design And Build Unique Landscapes For People Who Love The Outdoors". It really depends on the company's unique positioning and what they're the best at - but you get the point.

It's not at all about the products and services themselves. It's really about allowing the visitor to know almost immediately that you can help them with what they're looking for. When you do this right, they'll be willing to continue moving through your website and are much more likely to engage with you.

Coming up with this message takes time and some focused energy - and in many cases it can be a joint effort. It will be important to nail this down before we go into the build out stage of your site.

If you need some additional guidance or help with this, you can always reach out to us directly. We geek out on creating compelling messages for different markets, and it's often useful to have an outside perspective.

Once you have your clear message, you'll want to make sure that you also clarify exactly what it is you want a visitor to *do* once they've found your site. Because the goal of your website is to move the *right* prospects to becoming a customer.

And to do that, you'll need them to take action.

We work with a lot of clients that had previously thought that the job of their website was to provide information. And although that's true - what's most important - is that your website *moves* people to becoming your customer. And to do this, you need to guide the visitors to take action.

You need to make it abundantly clear what you want them to do.

And you need to make it incredibly easy for them to do it.

That's it.

You should have a clear call-to-action on every page of your site (the same action), and you should make it very easy to complete.

Now every business is different, but there are a few 'typical' calls to action that we deploy with our clients that cover about 90+ percent of the cases we run into. Here they are:

You can ask your prospects to call you; to complete a form

to get more information or to request something (a quote, a free sample etc.); to book an appointment; to buy something; to opt-in for something (a case study, white-paper or report etc.); to register for an event.

Like I said, there are more, but these cover most cases.

The first thing to do is look at your business, and determine the single most important job of your website. As an example, if your an e-commerce brand and sell products directly online (let's say you sell jewelry), then you might suspect that your website's primary job is to sell products. And although that's the end goal - you may have found that you can convert 2x as many people into buying a necklace when you can provide them a discount - and you also know that you can sell to more people, more frequently, if they're subscribed to your email newsletter that sends out monthly specials and unique, timely, holiday pieces.

Looking at the business website from this perspective, you'd probably determine that the best call to action would be to give someone a 10% off coupon code in exchange for their email address. Here's an example of how you could present this:

"Claim your instant 10% discount now! Plus, you'll be subscribed to our Members Only VIP Newsletter which includes special discounts and early access to our limited holiday special releases every month! Just let us know where to send the coupon code. Enter your email here: (and then a simple opt-in form).

They opt-in for the code and your CRM immediately emails it to them and subscribes them to your newsletter. It's a win-win for everyone.

In this way, not only do you increase initial conversions with the coupon code, you also add every new customer to your newsletter, and are in a position to sell them more in your monthly promotions. And for those that register for the code, but still don't buy (yes, there will be a number of these people) - you can still send them offers each month and eventually sell to them as well.

It costs a lot to get a new visitor to your website (in time and/or money depending on your business model), so you absolutely want to be maximizing the results you get from every visit. This is why you need to determine the single most effective call to action for your business, and make it the focus of your website. Get as many people as possible to take that 'first step' with you.

In the case above - for those wondering - yes, you can absolutely be sure to only show that offer to your first time visitors and/or non-customers if you choose. For everyone else, the call to action can be to something different - like to "Check out this week's specials" or to "Shop our most popular items" - depends on your business and goals - but you get the point.

The main thing here is to remember - you must take the time to figure out the single most important goal of your business website - and you must make sure you're directing every new visitor to take that action. And make it easy (and rewarding), for them to do what you're asking!

So, now that you have a single, powerful call to action across your site, it will be important to start thinking about what metrics to monitor once your site is live, so that you know the website is working to grow your business.

So let's talk very quickly about metrics.

Many small businesses will launch their website, and never monitor it.

This is a huge mistake.

I recommend checking in on your website's performance at

least once a month - so you can make sure it's bringing in new business, and increasing awareness for your company.

We'll talk later about how to make sure as many people as possible see your site each month (qualified, potential customers - not just random visitors) - so that makes this even more important.

Most businesses don't track their sites, because they simply don't know what to track - or how to track it. I'm going to simplify things for you right now.

When it comes to paid traffic - things are a little different, and the tools you'll use to drive things like Google Ads, Facebook Ads etc. can (and absolutely should), be set up to report exact conversions and goals independently. In these cases, you'll use dedicated reports to measure their performance.

But what about everything else?

Every website should have Google Analytics installed on it - no excuses. If you're unfamiliar, just do a Google search for "Google Analytics" and you can learn more. It's a free platform, that can give you incredibly important information about your website's performance, its visitors, and their behavior.

Because it is so robust, it can also be quite overwhelming for many users; but I'd encourage you not to get too "in the weeds" with it. For most small businesses, the default settings and reports will get you everything you need to make smart decisions.

Once your site is live, and it's installed, you can just sit back and let it collect the data you need.

The real work here for you, isn't all of the technical stuff - it's more about determining what your most important metrics are *first* - and then figuring out how you'll report on them.

These metrics are known as KPIs (Key Performance Indicators), and I'm a huge fan of "less is more" in this area. If reporting on your metrics is cumbersome or a task you (or a team member), will loath, then it's probably going to slowly fall by the wayside. And that will lead to reduced performance from your site over time. More importantly - it will leave an opening for your competitors to sneak in and steal more of that limited customer traffic each month.

We don't want that.

So, you need to figure out the 3-5 most important metrics to track that will let you know if your online performance (not just the website itself), is getting better, or worse, over time.

In the previous example, I might suggest we track the following KPIs:

1. Total online sales for the month (revenue).
2. Total number of orders placed for the month.
3. The average value of an order for the month.
4. Number of new subscribers (and coupon codes claimed), for the month.
5. Total visitors to the site for the month (broken out by new and returning visitors).

This would of course require additional discussion but it's a good place to start as an example.

You can see this gives me a good overview of the key areas for improvement (total sales, order value, results from primary calls to action, and overall traffic). I'd look at these numbers each month, then always be working to improve them. It's more about the trend of these numbers than the numbers themselves.

That's all on this topic - but the main point is this: what gets measured, improves. So start measuring just as soon as your site goes live!

As always, if you're just not sure about the best KPIs for your business - get in touch. We can help you figure them out. Each business is unique, but at the end of the day - we've worked in enough different industries and with enough different businesses, that I can confidently say - it's very likely we've helped another business that's not too different than yours - and we can make sure you're moving in the right direction with these incredibly important decisions.

Everything we're discussing here has long term implications, so it's important to get it right before we start with the build out.

Ok, that's everything for this stage.

You should now have a clear one-liner ready to be prominently displayed on your website. It should immediately answer the "what we do" and the "why we're better (or unique)" questions, and it should indicate to the reader that their life will be better in some way when they do business with you. That means it should clearly relay the problem you can (and will), solve for them, and it should stir some form of emotion from them whenever possible. Always remember - even in a business to business environment, you are always dealing with people. You should always be speaking to an individual.

You should also have a clearly defined and planned out call to action for your site - and have thought through the best way to make sure it is prominently displayed everywhere across your site. You should have made sure it's perfectly in alignment and supporting (even driving), your business growth goals.

And you should have determined how (and what), you're going to track with your website to make sure it's constantly improving, and working to grow your business.

Excellent.

You've done an amazing job to get to this point, and you've already put yourself in a position to outperform a large percentage of your competition. In the next few stages, you're going to learn how to position yourself for becoming the leader.

I hope you're ready to experience what it feels like to dominate your online space.

So, without further adieu, let's move on to the next stage of the Super Site process, where we'll actually start building out your site.

This is where most agencies or web designers *start*.

And that's why most websites don't grow your business. But yours will :)

5

BUILDING YOUR SUPER SITE - ALL OF THE THINGS YOU DIDN'T EVEN KNOW YOU DON'T KNOW

And now it's time to actually start building out your site.

Now, this isn't a book on becoming a professional web designer, so I'm not going to teach you how to install Wordpress or how to code PHP to customize your themes etc. Instead, this section is going to cover all of the things that will allow your website to outperform your competition.

I'm going to discuss those things that will allow your site to rank better, faster - because that's what really matters.

I'm going to cover the 'phases' of website build outs that we go through with all of our clients, and that we recommend you go through regardless of who is building out your site.

A few words of caution before we get started:

First of all, I don't ever recommend the use of a "do-it-yourself" website tool. I won't call any out specifically, but the reality is, those tools will never allow you to position your site as a true workhorse for growing the business. All of these tools are designed with the greatest focus on ease of use - not on building a site that will drive revenue, get ranked, and bring in new business.

A lot of solopreneurs will use a tool like this when they're working out of their basement or a back office at the house, but as soon as their business gets any real traction through local marketing and word of mouth efforts, they quickly realize their do-it-yourself website is little more than a placeholder for their business name online. It's better than nothing, but it's not going to move the needle.

We routinely rebuild websites for companies that got their start on one of these tools, and the results are always the same. As soon as we push our Super Sites live and it replaces their old "built with a website builder" website - they immediately (and for the first time ever), start seeing new, *inbound* leads and customers from the web. Save yourself the hassle and time messing with a do-it-yourself solution and simply build it right the first time.

Over the last decade, we've experimented with nearly every type of website solution, and for the vast majority of our clients we suggest WordPress as the framework - built out on your own domain and hosted on high performance cloud servers.

Currently we're hosting all of our client sites on Google's cloud hosting, and it is phenomenal. As you'll learn a bit later in this section - speed matters.

For larger e-commerce brands selling more than 10k products we do advise other platforms, but these are rare cases, and there are good reasons for needing custom built solutions at that scale.

That being said, self hosted WordPress build outs are the best solution for the vast majority of small businesses. It's completely customizable, easy to use and manage, is supported by a huge community of avid professionals, is open source, and the framework itself is free to use.

It is also one of the most secure platforms available, and is constantly being updated.

At the time of writing this, roughly thirty-five percent of the internet is powered by WordPress, and many of the top 100 sites in the *world* use it.

The point with all of this, is that it's incredibly stable; has been tested in the most severe environments; and is trusted by companies both large and small. WordPress works, and isn't going away. That can't be said for many other solutions that come and go.

So, we recommend a self hosted install of WordPress.

The other point to cover here is about hosting.

A lot of clients we speak with early on, don't realize the importance of quality hosting. They are often set up on shared hosting accounts, or low cost hosting. And this can be problematic.

I don't want to get too technical here, but there are a few important things to consider when choosing a hosting environment. First, be sure to pick an environment that specializes in WordPress hosting - it will make your life a lot easier when starting a build out.

You also want to make sure you choose a service that allows one-click setup of a staging environment, provides ssl certificates so your site stays secure, and (very important), hosting that is lightning fast. Slow loading sites don't rank as well as those that load quickly - and your hosting plays a big part in that.

There are other considerations as well, but the one most worth mentioning is the level of support you receive. You want to make sure whoever is hosting your site is responsive, and understands the need for your site to be online 24x7.

We currently host all of our client sites on the Google Cloud Platform, for ultimate performance, and we have a team dedicated to close to real-time support for our hosting clients. And it's much more affordable than you might think.

My only recommendation on hosting is to never compromise on quality hosting.

Remember, your business website is being designed to become your single biggest source of new customers - but it has to be set up properly. And quality hosting is a big part of that.

Ok, so we discussed our recommendations for platform and hosting - it's time to get into the actual build out process we use and recommend.

Let's get started.

Developing a Super Site (or any website for that matter), is typically a collaborative experience that involves working with a team of designers, developers, copywriters, project managers and you. It's also a very visual experience - meaning most business owners have a rough idea of what they like, but it's typically easier to make decisions when you can see that ideas and concepts that are being discussed.

Because of this, the foundation of all website projects start with a staging environment. This is basically a non-public environment where you can see exactly what your live website will be. You don't ever want to start building out a website on a live environment. There are lots of reasons for this, but the biggest two are:

1. You don't want to send Google false signals about your business, and as websites are being built out, there is typically a lot of placeholder information and/or poorly formatted content, images, menus etc. - we don't want to push that content live and have Google (or any search engine), misjudge your business and what you do or offer. This is very important. And.

2. We don't want a prospective customer to see an in-progress version of your business website - it just looks very unprofessional.

As I mentioned, there are many other reasons to work from a staging environment (especially for e-commerce businesses), but these two alone are enough.

So basically, when we work with a new client on their website build out (or redesign), the process is very simple, and usually goes like this:

1. We have a Discovery Meeting to discuss our shared visions of what the Super Site will look like and how it will be laid out. This happens after all of our research is complete, so we already know the competition we're up against and how we're going to show up differently etc. - so this is about website layout, design, menu placement, integrations etc.

2. Once we have an agreed upon plan, our design team works to bring that plan to life and creates a mock-up of the Super Site homepage (and sometimes additional pages depending on the project).

3. Once the mock-ups are complete, we then review with them with you (the client), and fine tune them to make sure we're all 100% on the same page and thrilled with the layout and design, messaging, calls to action etc.

4. With the mock-ups agreed upon, we get to work turning the vision into a fully functioning website. While the development team is working on building out your business's Super Site, we will likely have other team members working with you

to capture additional photography for your business or products, or creating videos for your business etc. Any additional marketing assets that are needed for the Super Site project are created, edited and prepped during this time.

5. Once the development team has everything built out, we typically have a final review of the site on the staging environment before going live.

6. Once everything is to your complete satisfaction, only then do we migrate the site to your live business domain. This is when it will be publicly visible to the world, and begin working for your business.

7. During the 'going live' stage, we will also secure the site, implement and test all tracking and analytics, optimize the site for speed, and perform an initial round of tests to make sure a new visitors experience will work as expected. This all happens within the first 2-4 hours of the site being live.

From a 30k foot view, that's the entire process. A typical Super Site planning and build out process normally takes less than 30 days.

The process is fun and exciting because you can see not only that you're building a strong, stand-out online presence for your business, but also because you know that it's part of a plan to grow your business - not just to be a placeholder for your business name online.

Getting the site planned, built and pushed live is in fact one of the biggest parts of the project - and doing it right is of course one of the most important parts - but it's not the only part.

Now that your site is live, it's time to make sure you're

getting it in front of the right people and showing up where people are looking for you.

It's time to start setting up your critical visibility campaigns.

"Stopping advertising to save money is like stopping your watch to save time."

– HENRY FORD

6

HOW TO MAKE SURE YOUR IDEAL CUSTOMERS SEE YOUR SITE EVERYWHERE AND EVERY TIME

Alright – it's about to get exciting now!

So, you've done the hard work of making sure your business can stand as a true competitor in the online space for your business. Your website is built, live and ready to start generating new business.

Excellent.

Now it's time to make sure your business is front and center and showing up on page one every time someone searches for one of your primary keywords.

When it comes to generating new business from the internet, there are primarily two types of advertising that come into play – interruptive advertising, and intent driven advertising.

Every business is unique, but as a general rule, we recommend you start investing in showing up where people are displaying 'buyer intent' – meaning they're going to a search engine, and typing in something that indicates they're in search for the products and/or services your company offers – i.e., they're looking to buy or schedule service etc.

If you've been looking at how to advertise your business online, you've probably discovered that there are hundreds (literally), of different ways to get exposure online. The reality is, the majority of these methods deliver very little (if any), results – and in some cases, they only work well within specific markets, or to specific audiences etc. It's easy to get confused or overwhelmed if you're not 'in the business'.

Here's the reality: In all of the markets we've worked in, and with all of the businesses we've helped scale, the vast majority (as in, almost all), generate nearly all of their results from 4 traffic streams – and I'm going to share those with you here.

Remember – we talked about the fact that there are only so many people going online each month and looking for the products and services your business offers each month (people showing 'buyer intent').

The primary goal is to get in front of 100% of these users.

As a secondary effort, we'll also try to get in front of people who aren't actively searching for your products and/or services, but who might show an interest if you can get in front of them (interruptive advertising). This is (in most cases), a secondary goal, however.

First and foremost we'll focus on getting in front of those people who are raising their hand and showing signs that they could use your help! This is what we call the 'low hanging fruit', and it's where you'll generate the greatest results and how you'll be able to grow your business the fastest.

Ok, so let's get right into it.

For most businesses, as you can imagine, your greatest opportunity is to show up as high on the front page of Google as possible, for relevant searches for your business – of course. But you also want to show up in as many *placements* as possible.

Businesses that are crushing it with the internet typically own *multiple* spots on page one of Google for their primary keywords. Depending on your business, there are different placements available, but let's use our Four Seasons Landscaping LLC business as an example.

For a local service business like this, there are at least three placements available on page one. There are the Google Ads at the very top of the page, the Google My Business (GMB), Listings in the middle of the page, and then there are the Organic Listings on the lower third of the page. Our most successful clients will do the following as a minimum:

1. You'll be running Google Ads (top of page placements) for your business name and primary keywords. You'll only be running those ads in the locations that you service (geo-targeting), and you'll make sure someone is always picking up the phone to capture and convert interested leads – this is a must. If you don't pick up the phone, you've set a bad initial experience for these visitors, and they'll call the next listing on Google.

2. You'll also be running Remarketing campaigns for everyone who showed an interest in your business by clicking an ad or visiting your website. The reality is – customers nowadays will explore their options, and compare your business against the competition (that's why we start with a stand-out website), so you need to make sure they're seeing *your* business even when they're looking at your competition and/or surfing the web.

3. If you're a service based business, then the Google Business Listings (also known as the 'Maps Listings'), will be another critical driver for new business. These are the listings you typically see in the middle of the search results page – often they're boxed out and stand out on the page. Typically only 3-4 listings are shown, and then there's a 'show more businesses' link that allows people to research a bit more. The top listings get the vast majority of visits, so you want to do everything possible to optimize your listing, and to drive positive business reviews (these show up prominently in the listings, and are a ranking factor). Getting a top placement in this area can drive significant new business for you, so it's worth the investment.

4. Lastly, you want to make sure your website is optimized to show up in the 'Organic' listings for page one. This is known as Search Engine Optimization (SEO), and is an important part of any online visibility campaign. The Organic listings are shown below the Google Business Listings if they are present. If there are no business listings for your industry, then these organic listings show up directly below the paid ads, and are even more important.

As you can see, by focusing on these key areas for the most important terms to your business, you'll be able to own 3 or more positions on page one. Showing up in multiple placements acts as a multiplier effect. It increases confidence for searchers that you're a great business to work with. Having a strong presence like this builds trust for your company even before the prospect calls, or shops with you. People see every placement as a 'vote' from Google that you're the best choice when it comes to the products/services they're searching out. And people trust Google.

Every business has a limited marketing budget, and it's not always possible to 'own' all of these positions at once. You have to remember however – this is an investment in your business. The goal isn't to spend money to optimize these placements and to get this exposure without a return. Our goal for all clients is always to see a positive return on investment in advertising.

You'll notice that your biggest competitors are typically showing up in multiple places on page one. A lot of newer/in-experienced businesses think that they are able to show up in so many places because they're a big company and have tons of money to invest in marketing – but the reality is that they are a successful company *because* they invest in advertising and are showing up as the best choice to do business with.

The companies that invest in a strong online presence are the ones that are going to be here for the long term. Those that don't invest in showing up (and showing up the right way), when people are searching for the products/services they offer online are not likely to survive.

Businesses grow *because* of successful marketing and positioning – it's *not* the other way around.

And let's not forget about Facebook.

Facebook advertising is an incredible traffic stream and/or conversion booster for many businesses. Facebook is an 'interruptive' form of advertising (in almost all cases). People aren't usually searching out businesses on Facebook. They may ask friends for recommendations etc., but they're not doing research on their options on Facebook. They're there for the social experience – so you have to show up the right way.

For the majority of our local business clients we use Facebook as a strong remarketing platform, and as a Brand Awareness tool. It works incredibly well in these ways and can drive significant new business when coupled with the traffic strategies we reviewed above. This is called multi-channel marketing, and it is a must for any successful advertising campaign.

As a quick aside: a lot of businesses we talk with believe that they need someone posting content on their Facebook pages etc. The reality is, the days of Facebook showing your organic content are gone. If you want your message/business to be seen – you'll have to pay for it to be promoted. You should certainly have great content, images, reviews etc. on your Business Page, but don't expect people to find you organically. There are just too many advertisers willing to pay to show up in the Facebook user's feeds, so there's no room left for Facebook to share your business content organically (for free). That being said - Facebook ads are a great, cost effective marketing channel and a good investment when used strategically and in a 'cool' way.

So now you know where to focus with the majority of your online marketing efforts.

Remember, the goal is to get your new site to show up (as prominently as possible), every time a prospect is searching out the products/services you offer.

Knowing that your business likely has a limited marketing budget – how do you know where to invest first? Well, the good news is that it's not too hard to determine. Every business is unique, and we recommend having a more in-depth meeting to outline a specific plan for your business, but as a general rule (this applies to about 80% of businesses we meet with), the order we recommend tackling these advertising channels is:

1. Google Ads - Get to the top of page one fast. Besides near immediate visibility, you'll only show up for the search queries you specify to Google – meaning you can choose to show up for only those terms that are likely to lead to the most profitable new business. And remember, you only pay Google when they deliver a visitor to your site - this gets you in the game quickly and affordably.

2. Remarketing - You want to make sure once you've got a visitor to your site, that you continue to show up for them as they continue to browse the web – preferably until they become a customer. Don't let your competition steal them away!

3. Google Business Listings - This is an excellent source of ongoing traffic for your website and calls to your business. These listings should be optimized as soon as possible (we often work on these alongside running Google Ads). You'll want to get as many reviews as possible on these listings as well. We can help you automate this process and streamline the way you get positive reviews from your current and new customers/clients. As an aside – don't ever try to get fake reviews – Google will know, and they'll ban your business – permanently.

4. Search Engine Optimization (SEO) - We move to SEO next, because it's a longer term strategy. It can take 3-6 months to see your initial investment in SEO start paying off. Many clients are looking for a blend of immediate results and long term strategy. When we build the site out initially, we do a solid foundational SEO pass on the site, so this sets us up

perfectly to launch the advanced SEO strategies 30-60 days after site launch. SEO is often one of the most profitable forms of online visibility for clients and allows you to pick up additional page one placements for your core keywords. Many new clients don't understand the 'multiplier' effect showing up in multiple spots on page one can have. Clients are typically shocked to see their Google Ads costs often decreasing once their organic placements start moving up the page. They will also see higher Click through rates on all placements, and their combined efforts start to have a positive snowball effect on the growth of the business.

5. Facebook - Once we're underway with the intent driven marketing channels, we suggest immediately adding Facebook campaigns to the mix – especially as it relates to remarketing.

It's an exciting time to see your new website slowly start dominating your market. Because you've done the proper foundational groundwork, your website is designed to convert more visitors than your competition – meaning you'll have more money to put back into the advertising campaigns, and fuel your business.

In a short period of time, *your* business will be the one everyone sees when going online and searching for the products/services you offer. It's an exciting journey – and seeing the change it makes in the businesses we work with – and in the lives of the ownership and staff of these businesses is what drives us in all that we do.

I can't wait for you to experience it for yourself.

So that covers the online visibility campaigns that will allow you to move to a position of market dominance in the shortest period of time, for the smallest investment; with no confusion, and no wasted revenue.

Let's talk quickly about how to monitor results, growth and scaling next.

7

MOVING TOWARD MARKET DOMINATION (OR JUST MAKING A BUNCH MORE MONEY - YOUR CHOICE)

Your Super Site is live; your traffic campaigns have been launched; and Google has been sent all of the necessary 'signals' to alert them that you're a contender for the keywords that mean the most to your business.

Hopefully you've had your Google Business page optimized, have launched a small Google Ads campaign, and have an SEO strategy planned. Not all businesses will utilize all of these strategies right out of the gate, and that's completely fine. The most important part is that you start with *something*, and that you have a plan.

This is where the magic happens.

All that's required is a little patience and some active management of your newly launched traffic campaigns.

For most new clients we work with, this is what the Super Site post-launch timeline looks like:

1. First 30 Days - We've launched a small Google Ads campaign, and the business is showing top of page for all branded keywords. You're also showing up

prominently for those terms that we've agreed are *most* important to your business. We've typically also claimed, optimized and linked your GMB page to your website, and your inbound traffic from that source will start to see a gradual increase during this first month. For client's running Google Ads, we will normally send a 2-week check in from the time the campaigns have gone live, and then we will do a 30 day in-person meeting (phone, video conference, or in-office – whichever is most convenient for you), where we break down what's working well; what we're working on improving; and what we will be adjusting in the next 30 day window. The first 90 days of a paid traffic campaign are critical, so we typically meet once a month during this window to review and keep things on track for scaling.

2. Days 31-90 - You should start to see a small uptick in your Organic ('free'), traffic from your Super Site as a result of the foundational work we put in during the build out. This can take a little longer for brand new domains, as Google typically puts you in the 'sandbox' (a state where Google watches your website, and crawls it, but won't actually rank, or show it in the listings), for anywhere from 3-6 months. This allows Google time to watch your site for activity, social signals etc. to make sure you're credible, and worthy to present to their users. In our experience, running Google Ads is a good way to shorten this time period for new properties. This is because Google can use user behavior data (such as time on site, conversions etc.), from the traffic you're sending to the site through Google Ads.

Many times (for new businesses), this alone is a good enough reason to start running Google Ads right away. During this month two/three window your results from Google Ads and your Google Business Listing should be improving. This means more leads and more consistency – and when it comes to Google Ads, the leads will be getting lower in cost and higher in volume. It's exciting to see everything moving toward greater efficiency. We're typically doing a monthly check in with you during this critical time.

3. Days 91 and beyond - At this point, we have a fairly smooth running Google Ads account. We're doing daily check-ins on the account of course (looking for any issues and opportunities), but we're also running our proprietary 15-point account optimization process on a weekly basis. Doing so ensures sure your account maintains its well earned quality score (which affects your cost for every click). Google likes to see accounts that are being actively managed following their best practices. They reward you as an advertiser with higher quality clicks at a lower cost. We've got your back here! Also, at the 90+ day mark, our SEO campaigns are normally well underway, and you're starting to see more organic traffic, and more inquiries coming from these placements. You'll likely be seeing more and more first page placements for not only your core keywords, but also for other similar terms. This is the point where you really start to see the impact of a well built website coupled with a well-run traffic campaign.

It's all about scaling from here.

Having a website that brings in a lot of new business for you is great, but we'd be remiss if we didn't take just a moment to discuss responsible scaling. We *love* being able to solve our client's online appearance, visibility and lead flow problems – that's why we designed the Super Site process. However, we only work with clients who deliver amazing services and/or products – that's important to us. The last thing we want to do is help a sub-par business steal market share from competitors who would deliver a better user experience.

Given that, we normally screen our clients early on to ensure they provide amazing products/services, at fair prices – and that they provide a great customer experience. As you can imagine, increasing new customer flow does put additional (and often unfamiliar), pressures on good businesses. So the only thing we ask of our client's is that they have a plan for maintaining an amazing customer experience even with the increased lead flow.

We want this to be an amazing experience for not only the new customer, but also for *you*, the business owner or leader. Increasing your growth rate will no doubt introduce new problems in the business. These are the best types of problems a business could ask for, but we want to make sure you've thought about the upside of all of this and the effects it will have on your ability to 'keep up'.

If your desire is to be the most prominent business in your industry, and to be one of the busiest, most recognized names in your market, then the Super Site process is going to be a perfect fit for you.

If you're just looking to grow a little bit, or to maintain a certain level of business, then we can help with that, and the process will work; but we need to know up front. We'll adjust (dial down), the plan based on your individual needs.

It's just really important to be clear about your desires right out of the gate.

Our only goal is for this to be an amazing experience for you, your business, your staff, and all of the people that are about to find you online.

"The future depends on what you do today."

- MAHATMA GANDHI

8

WHEN, WHY AND HOW TO START

First off, I want to thank you for taking the time to read the Super Site book. My only goal has been to help you, as a small business owner (or a person responsible for the growth of a small business), to get a handle on the best way to launch (or redesign), your business website and your online presence.

I've seen these techniques work wonders, time and time again for businesses of all shapes and sizes - and I know it can help yours as well.

We're passionate about helping NH's Small Businesses grow - period. It's what drives everything we do.

So, before we part ways, I want to answer three final questions I hear from time to time - and here they are:

1. When should I start? This one is simple to answer, and it's the same for every business no matter where you're at in the growth curve. Get started *now!* The reality is that the internet is getting more and more competitive every single day, and the more time you give your competition to stake their

claim, the harder it's going to be for you to catch up. The later you start, the more time and money it's going to take to catch up. Businesses who delay building a strong online presence are likely to fade away in the coming decade. It doesn't matter what industry you're in; who your ideal prospect is; or where you think they're hanging out. I guarantee you, your strongest competitors (those planning to be around for the long haul), are securing their position online. Get started today. As a matter of fact, the *best* time to get started is when you think you're *already* too busy. Some of these strategies take time to deploy and start yielding fruit. Get them started when your livelihood isn't dependent on immediate results!

2. Why should I choose the Super Site model - won't a regular website do? If you've read this far, you already know the answer to this, so I won't waste anyone's time by restating the obvious. But I do want to answer "Why should you choose NH Strategic Marketing?" Well, to start with, the Super Site Process is *ours*. We literally wrote the book on building website *systems* that grow businesses. It's what we do and we're without question the absolute best at it. Spend 15 minutes talking with us at our downtown Concord, NH office and you'll agree - I'm sure of it. And that brings us to the last question...

3. How do I get stared? It couldn't be easier. Visit our website at https://NHStrategicMarketing.com and either give us a call or submit an inquiry through the site. We'll set up a time to do a complimentary Discovery Meeting and during this meeting you'll

discover *exactly* how we would go about designing and improving your online visibility. There's no charge for this consultation, and by the end of the meeting, we'll be able to determine if it make sense for us to work together.

We're a zero pressure agency, so don't worry about getting pushed into making snap decisions or hard sold - that's not how we operate.

Our company motto is "do the right thing" and we believe in treating others as we ourselves would like to be treated.

Of course, I encourage you to check out our 5-star Google and Facebook ratings. At the time of writing this book, we have more positive reviews than any other agency in NH. You can also look us up through the Better Business Bureau.

Oh, and if you live in or around Concord, NH then you can probably just ask around about us - most business leaders in the area are familiar with our work and team - we've probably helped someone you know in some way already.

I hope to speak with you soon. And until then, I wish you the greatest of success with your business.